THE UNEXPLAINED

UFOs

BY DAVE WENCEL

BELLWETHER MEDIA · MINNEAPOLIS, MN

Are you ready to take it to the extreme?
Torque books thrust you into the action-packed world
of sports, vehicles, mystery, and adventure. These books
may include dirt, smoke, fire, and dangerous stunts.
WARNING: read at your own risk.

Library of Congress Cataloging-in-Publication Data

Wencel, Dave.
 UfOs / by Dave Wencel.
   p. cm. -- (Torque. The unexplained)
 Includes bibliographical references and index.
 Summary: "Engaging images accompany information about UFOs. The combination of high-
interest subject matter and light text is intended for students in grades 3 through 7"--Provided
by publisher.
 ISBN 978-1-60014-504-9 (hardcover : alk. paper)
 1. Unidentified flying objects--Juvenile literature. I. Title.
TL789.2.W445 2010
 001.942--dc22   2010011406

This edition first published in 2011 by Bellwether Media, Inc.

Printed in the United States of America, North Mankato, MN.

080110   1162

CONTENTS

CHAPTER 1
INCIDENT AT ROSWELL

S omething strange happened in
Roswell, New Mexico on July 2, 1947.
People saw a glowing object streak
across the sky. They also heard a large explosion.
The next morning, a local rancher found some
mysterious **wreckage** on the ground.

Officer Irving Newton goes through the wreckage from Roswell that he claims is from a weather balloon.

The rancher reported the objects he found to the local sheriff. The United States Army had an air base nearby. Base officials heard about the report. They came out and took the wreckage. The Army released a statement a few days later. It said that they had recovered a disc. The Army later changed their statement. They now claim the wreckage was a crashed **weather balloon**.

Some people believe that more than just UFO wreckage is kept at Area 51. They think the government has alien bodies there too!

ALIENS UNDER WRAPS

WARNING
AREA 51
Restricted Area

It is unlawful to enter this area without permission of the Installation Commander.
Sec.21, International Security Act of 1950; 50 U.S.C.797

While on this installation all personnel and the property under their control are subject to search.

USE OF DEADLY FORCE AUTHORIZED

AREA 51

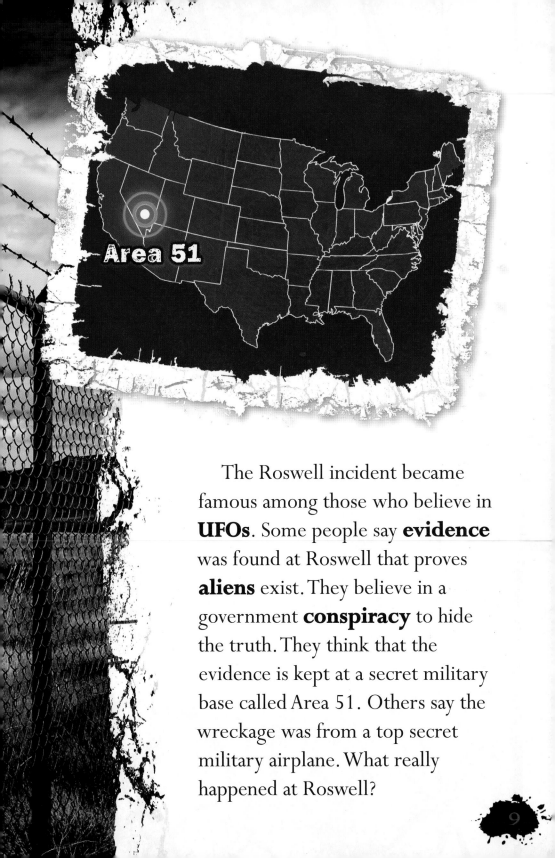

Area 51

The Roswell incident became famous among those who believe in **UFOs**. Some people say **evidence** was found at Roswell that proves **aliens** exist. They believe in a government **conspiracy** to hide the truth. They think that the evidence is kept at a secret military base called Area 51. Others say the wreckage was from a top secret military airplane. What really happened at Roswell?

CHAPTER 2
WHAT ARE UFOs?

ABDUCTION!

Many people claim to have been taken, or abducted, by aliens. They say that aliens have brought them aboard spacecraft to experiment on and study them.

U FO stands for "unidentified flying object." The term describes any unknown, moving object in the sky. It most often refers to a flying saucer or other alien aircraft.

People have been reporting strange objects in the sky for hundreds of years. Some UFOs appear as sets of lights moving across the sky. Others are reported as flying saucers.

Project Blue Book staff

The United States government set up Project Blue Book in 1952 to study UFO sightings. Researchers collected and examined 12,618 UFO reports from 1952 to 1970. They looked into possible explanations to determine whether UFOs were visiting Earth. There have been thousands of reports since then. Could any of these prove that aliens have come to our planet?

HISTORY OF THE MYSTERY

Year	Place
1947	Washington State
1947	New Mexico
1952	United States
1957	Texas
1961	New Hampshire
1969	Oklahoma
1997	Arizona
2006	Illinois
2007	Hawaii

Event

Pilot Kenneth Arnold sees nine strange objects moving at high speeds across the sky.

Something crashes outside of Roswell, New Mexico; the U.S. military recovers the wreckage.

The U.S. government starts Project Blue Book to study UFO sightings; more than 1,500 sightings are reported that year.

Many witnesses report a mysterious object near Levelland, Texas; they claim the object caused their vehicles to shut off.

Betty and Barney Hill claim to have been abducted by aliens; their abduction report is the first of its kind.

Future U.S. President Jimmy Carter sees a UFO while at a speech; he does not believe it to be an alien aircraft.

Thousands of people in Arizona and Nevada claim to see strange lights in the sky.

Twelve employees at Chicago's O'Hare airport report seeing a flying saucer over an airport gate.

News cameras record UFOs moving through the sky, even though no objects appear on radar.

CHAPTER 3
SEARCHING FOR ANSWERS

Venus

M any people are trying to explain UFOs.
Some people try to find proof that aliens are
visiting planet Earth. They set up cameras to
watch the night sky. They interview people who claim
to have seen UFOs. Dozens of organizations study
UFO sightings.

Most UFO sightings are easily explained. People have mistaken helicopters and planes for UFOs. The bright light of Venus often looks like a flying object. Weather balloons are also commonly reported as UFOs. Do these explanations cover all reports? Some people say no. They believe that UFOs and aliens have come to Earth.

weather balloon

Do these photos prove UFOs exist, or are they hoaxes?

Skeptics think that all UFO sightings can be explained. They claim that photos and reports of UFOs are **hoaxes**. They point out that no proof of an alien UFO has ever been found. However, no one can prove that a spaceship has not visited Earth.

ALIEN SIGNS?

For years, people have been finding large circles and other strange shapes in fields. Many believe these crop circles come from UFOs.

crop circle

Do UFOs bring aliens to Earth, or can all mysterious sightings of flying objects be explained? Maybe someday we will know for sure. Until then, we can only watch the sky.

GLOSSARY

aliens—beings from other planets

conspiracy—a secret agreement between two or more people to perform or hide an act or event

evidence—physical proof of something

hoaxes—attempts to trick people into believing something

skeptics—people who do not believe in something

UFOs—unidentified flying objects; objects in the sky that cannot be identified.

weather balloon—a large balloon that floats high in the atmosphere and takes weather readings

wreckage—the ruined remains of something, such as a crashed aircraft

TO LEARN MORE

AT THE LIBRARY

Grace, N.B. *UFO Mysteries*. Chanhassen, Minn.: Child's World, 2007.

Mason, Paul. *UFOs and Crop Circles*. North Mankato, Minn.: Smart Apple Media, 2005.

Nobleman, Marc Tyler. *Aliens and UFOs*. Chicago, Ill.: Raintree, 2007.

ON THE WEB

Learning more about UFOs is as easy as 1, 2, 3.

1. Go to www.factsurfer.com.

2. Enter "UFOs" into the search box.

3. Click the "Surf" button and you will see a list of related Web sites.

With factsurfer.com, finding more information is just a click away.

INDEX

The images in this book are reproduced through the courtesy of: NadyaPhoto, front cover; Jon Eppard, pp. 4-5, 10-11; Mary Evans/ Photo Researchers, Inc., pp. 6-7; M L Pearson/Alamy, p. 7 (small); Juan Martinez, pp. 8-9, 9 (small); Corbis/Photolibrary, pp. 12, 20-21; Mary Evans Picture Library/The Image Works, p. 13; Fred Goldstein, pp. 14-15; Baback Tafreshi/Photo Researchers, Inc., p. 16; David Parker/Photo Researchers, Inc., pp. 17, 19; Dale O'Dell/Alamy, p. 18 (top, bottom).